ONE NIGHT IN A ONE LIGHT TOWN

Short Stories and Long Memories

William Hanson Hammonds

ONE NIGHT IN A ONE LIGHT TOWN.
© 2007 by William Hanson Hammonds
All rights reserved

ISBN: 978-0-6151-4512-9

Printed in the United States of America.
No part of this book may be used or reproduced in any manner whatsoever without prior permission in writing from the author.

Cover art and design by Ashlee E. Hammonds

IN MEMORY

Bobby Wicks, Joe Grant, Glenn Harrell

Friends Along The Way...

ACKNOWLEDGMENTS

This book in many ways has become a team effort. Any author will tell you that writing a book is not a one person endeavor. There are many important people, more than I can mention here, who contributed significantly to my life as I was growing up in Crofton, Kentucky. Many of them were members of First Christian Church, where I joined the church at age fifteen. More recently, Eldon "Peabody" Pyle, George Pyle, Charlie Barnes and Billy Wagoner filled in the gaps of my memory as I composed these stories.

There were others who provided useful information about people, places, and dates. My thanks are expressed to Bill and Nell Lile, Paul Jones, Carl Taylor, Dr. Walter Bell and Larry Richardson.

Finally, I want to express my appreciation to my son and daughter-in-law, Matthew and Ashlee, for editing the manuscript and arranging a publisher for my book. It was that final push that led me to "get-er-done." Many thanks go to my entire family who was cheering for me on the sidelines!

I had a great time revisiting these stories. I really don't know why I was so reluctant to start writing. During the last forty-four years I guess I must have written at least twenty-five hundred sermons and speeches, but I have never written much about my own life. The idea of this book gave me that freedom.

FOREWORD

This book is the story of eight boys who grew up in a small town in Western Kentucky in the mid nineteen forties to early fifties. Today these men have enjoyed a camaraderie that has lasted more than sixty years. There are five living members of this group today. This book is filled with real, enjoyable adventures of growing up in a magical world.

The town in which we grew up was such a place every grown man would like to return to at least once in his lifetime. Memories are wonderful gifts that brighten our days and give a boost to life. Often memories can be fleeting but they usually return while climbing up a hill, or strolling down a lane, or looking over a ridge.

Memories also remind us that we grew up in a wonderful place called Childhood. For me that time and place are far away, but I can return anytime I choose in my memory. For me, it was a place of safety, a place where dreams were made and where many came true.

My life began back there with two beautiful people I called Parents. I lived with a small group called Family. I spent many of my days with a crowd called Friends. Now that I'm viewed as a senior citizen, I realize that old age is like a bank account. You can only withdraw on what you have deposited through the years. Thanks to these seven close friends, the experience of writing this book opens an account of memories that I can draw interest from for the rest of my life.

CONTENTS

One Night In A One Light Town	13
Short Stories and Long Memories	17
Seven Wonders of 'Our' World	21
The Play Park	37
A Typical Sunday in Crofton	41
School Daze	45
Teachers Remembered	47
Wild Weekend Escapades: Part I	51
Wild Weekend Escapades: Part II	53
Adventures in Driving	55
An Erstwhile Dating Experiment	59
Another Dating Experiment Gone Awry	61
Basketball Trivia: Crofton Cougars	63
Jobs Available to Youngsters from 1945-1950	67
Working Can Be Fun	71
Personalities	73
Nicknames	81
The Old Days	83

ONE NIGHT IN A ONE LIGHT TOWN

Short Stories and Long Memories

ONE NIGHT IN A ONE LIGHT TOWN

It was near dusk when Peabody, Bobby Wicks, George Pyle and I left the Eat Shop and headed toward the DX Service Station. We were all a bit pensive as we sat down on the "Loafers Bench", across the highway from the station. This was the last night in town for Eldon, Bobby and I before we left for the military the next morning. The date was October 12, 1951 and there was a chill in the air, or so it seemed.

Bobby spoke first, "Well, it's hard to imagine that this will be our last night together for maybe a long time." Peabody chimed in, "Well, it could be years. We don't know where we'll be going after basic training."

Bobby and I were going to Lackland Air Force Base in San Antonio, Texas. We would be with each other for the next eight weeks. Peabody was headed to a naval base in San Diego, California. I might have joined the Navy with Peabody, except I didn't like bell bottom trousers. The truth is, I didn't like the sea all that well either.

George was Peabody's younger brother, and too young to enlist. "I sure wish I was going with you guys," he said. Someone suggested we take a walk around town. We walked toward the Eat Shop and turned to the right at the one lone caution light that was swinging to and fro in the wind. This was the only traffic light in town. Motorists traveling up and down Highway 41 surely didn't like to slow down as they came through this small town. It was the only light in about ten miles.

None of us had ever been away from home for more than a week. We were all mostly homebodies. Now, three of us would likely be away at least four years, or perhaps longer. The route we were walking that evening was familiar to all of us. We had walked that way hundreds of times to school. But somehow it seemed different this time, quieter, longer. Our conversation had all but ceased as we continued our journey.

The scenery was as familiar to us as we were to one another. We passed the Shell station on the corner where we turned, and there was the barber shop on the corner. Our walk led us by Tyson's grocery store, where kids on their way home from school could stop and get a snack.

The town's only hotel was located in the middle of that block. The old hotel was built around 1918, but it was still an impressive structure, run by "Miss Hett" Twedell and her husband, Boyd. The railroad stretched through the middle of town and the hotel guests found that their dishes rattled when the train passed by. In the summer, when the windows were open, you could smell fried chicken cooking a block away. Two of our buddies, Elbert and Delbert Rhodes, lived there and attended Crofton High School.

The telephone office was just past the hotel on the right, a tiny building sitting almost on the sidewalk. The inside of the office wasn't much larger than a walk-in closet. I can recall the names of two of the telephone operators, Dimple McKnight and Eva Wells. A caller might ask the operator for number 316 or 430, or some other three digit number. There were a lot of party lines too, which meant there was more than one family on the line. This situation lent itself to people listening to the conversations of others, if they so desired.

The U.S. Post Office was the last building on that street. Dan Mitchell was the postmaster for many years. His daughter Sue worked in the office some when she was at home. Some of us were always kidding around with her. She was a good sport and spoke "pig Latin" as well as we did.

Our tour took us across the railroad by the L&N Depot, and the giant water tower that dispensed water to steam engines. Several of the businesses got their water there too, since Crofton had no city water at that time. Some of the daredevils in town occasionally scaled the high tower by a narrow ladder that ran from the ground to the top of the tower. I think it was probably the tallest structure in town. Parked alongside the Depot were three or four large wagons with long tongues. They were used to haul cargo of any kind to the merchants around town. A few of the businessmen pulled the wagons back to their stores by themselves. It was possible to pick up someone to do this for you for about fifty cents.

Our final leg of the trip took us by Punch Croft's Pool Room where we had spent many happy hours playing bank pool or nine ball, at ten cents a game. From there we passed by the old bank building and a grocery store. Further up the street were two dry goods stores owned by brothers, Ben and Frank Gordon. Traveling on we passed an ice cream parlor, and an old mill where one could buy a sack of cobs.

Turning left at the end of the street, we headed toward Crofton School. Originally all twelve grades met in this building, before the fire destroyed it in 1951. I was one of seventeen who graduated there the same year. As we looked around the old school where the gym used to be, we all said with one voice, "Let's crawl in through a window and shoot some basketball for one last time." It was, as Yogi Berra said, "Déjà vu all over again." After a while we decided to go home and spend what was left of the evening with our families.

It was a night to remember...

SHORT STORIES AND LONG MEMORIES

Everybody loves a good story, but not everybody can tell a good story. A story may be anecdotal, narrative, a tale or biography. Stories can be in part, historical, fiction, non-fiction or even legend. A story can be about the past, the present, or by a stretch of the imagination, the future. The short stories in this book are about things that happened in the past, repeated in the present, and hold the potential of being remembered in the future.

Often events that occurred in the past have a sense of mystery, whether they are true or false. I'm using the legendary story King Arthur and the Knights of the Round Table to serve as a launching pad for this collection of short stories about real people living in a real place. From Richard Burton's *Camelot*, we hear:

"...Let it not be forgot
That once there was a spot
For one brief shining moment
Known as Camelot."

Camelot was a famous castle in the medieval legend of King Arthur. King Arthur established a brilliant court and seated the greatest and most chivalrous warriors in Europe, the Knights of the Round Table. The actual location of Camelot remains unknown.

Perhaps it was a state of mind, a mythological spot gone forever…that is, until it emerged again in time and space in the western corner of Kentucky in a spot called Crofton. Several components found in the story of Camelot are missing in my stories. There is no King, no Knights, no Round Table and no Court.

Maybe there could have been a court, if a court can be defined as a gathering of individuals, or a quadrangular space that is marked off for games. Instead of searching for the Holy Grail, these eight young men searched for adventure and fun. During the course of events, friendships developed that would last throughout their lives.

During the post war years of the early forties, this modern Camelot (Crofton) was a thriving little hamlet of eight hundred people. The coal mining industry was the largest employer for many in town. Farming probably came in second place. Several smaller businesses were located there. The town supported a bank, a drug store, a restaurant or two, a hotel, a barber shop, pool hall, post office, ice cream parlor, grist mill, dry good stores, grocery stores, two service stations, a shoe repair shop, telephone office and a blacksmith shop among others.

The Company Store was probably the largest store in town. It was the main trading place for the coal miners who could charge their purchases and pay on them monthly. The store calls to mind the lyrics of Tennessee Ernie Ford's song, "Sixteen Tons."

"Well, you shovel sixteen tons
And whatta you get,
Another day older
And deeper in debt.

Saint Peter, don't you call me,
Cause I can't go;
I owe my soul,
To the Company Store."

Crofton was our Camelot, a wonderful place to raise a family. Have you ever wondered what it is that makes folks write and sing songs about the places where they were born? One such song was popular in the fifties. I believe the title was "Dear Hearts and Gentle People,"

I love those dear hearts and gentle people,
Who live in my home town.
Because those dear hearts and gentle people
Will never ever let you down.

I feel so welcome each time that I return
That my happy heart keeps laughin' like a clown.
I love the dear hearts and gentle people,
Who live and love in my home town.

No matter the size of the town where we grew up, we always like to go back for a visit whenever we can. Your home town is the nucleus of your life, the seed bed of your dreams and aspirations. There are distinguishing characteristics about such a place that you never forget, and with which you always identify it. For me, and at least seven best friends of mine, Crofton was that spot.

"...Let it not be forgot
That once there was a spot
For one brief shining moment
Known as Camelot."

SEVEN WONDERS OF 'OUR' WORLD

History tells us there were Seven Wonders of the World. Today only one of the ancient Wonders, the Great Pyramid of Giza, still exists. A non-profit Swiss foundation called "New 7 Wonders" is promoting a global voting campaign to name seven new wonders by July 7, 2007. The only criteria for the new list are that the landmarks were built or discovered before the year 2000. This leaves my list in the running. The seven landmarks I have listed played a great Part in our growing up years.

DX SERVICE STATION

DRIPPING SPRINGS

CROFTON LAKE

THE BLUFFS

PUNCH'S POOL HALL

CROFTON SCHOOL

THE EAT SHOP

THE DX SERVICE STATION

The DX was a service station on Highway 41 that ran right through town. The station sold gasoline, about fifteen cents a gallon at that time. It was also a garage that changed oil and filter. Cars were washed there also. The station was a terminal for the Greyhound Bus Station. You could purchase snacks, candy, and cold drinks.

A man with the illustrious name of Jesse James West was one of the attendants at the station. He was a polio victim, but managed to do his job and you could count on him to be at work every day. Dulin Crabtree was also an attendant at the station. He would write the bus schedule on a chalk board that was hanging on the wall. When someone asked about the schedule, he would always say, "Read the damn menu!"

Then there was the incomparable, master-of-all-things-automotive-attendant, "Pieface" Lloyd. I was never sure just what his job was, but he always walked around with a shop rag about six feet long, dragging on the ground behind him with a baseball cap sitting rakishly on his head. He personified professionalism at the highest level.

There was a wooden bench stationed across the highway from the DX. It was a bench put there for bus patrons who might want to sit down and wait on the bus. But someone had given it the name "Loafers' Bench." This seat was generally occupied in early morning and evening by older men. Some of the men were veterans of WWII, who liked to get together and swap stories, many of which were not true. Once, Sterling Lamb was talking about going overseas. He said he had been across the ocean five times. Some wise guy said if so, that would have left him on the other side.

The DX provided services for automobile and truck owners, as well as selling Greyhound Bus tickets. It also served as a haven for kids to hang out in the afternoons and evenings. But the DX was more than that. It was an historical landmark, not because it was located there for eons, but because of the historical happenings over the years.

As newlyweds, my wife, Carolyn, and I, lived in the old Burkholder House across the highway from the DX. Bobby and Nancy Adams, also newlyweds, lived in one of the apartments. We lived on the highway side facing the station. On weekends there was always a lot of activity at the station. On Saturday night, after we had gone to bed, we used to open our window blinds so we could have a grand view of the station.

It seemed there was always more traffic after midnight, with an occasional wreck. Fist fights were more likely to occur after midnight. It was like being parked on the front row at a drive-in, watching an action movie. Sometimes we would have popcorn and a double cola, while we watched what was happening. It was a wonderful time when the world was young, and so were we. The DX appeared as one of the wonders of our world.

DRIPPING SPRINGS

Dripping Springs....it's easy to see how the name came about. During the rainy season, there was for many years, water dripping down into a low place that turned into a swimming hole. While it couldn't be compared to the Hanging Gardens of Babylon, built by King Nebuchadnezzar on the banks of the Euphrates River, it has become legendary in the lives of many kids who learned to swim there.

A few years ago while attending my high school reunion, I made a side trip to Dripping Springs. Strange how big it used to look when I was a boy, and how small it looked as I stood on its banks. I was reminded of an old adage that says, "The older a man gets, the farther he walked to school when he was a boy." But as I stood there at the edge of the swimming hole, my mind took a journey backward in time. There were so many memories that flooded my mind. Suddenly they were all there: Glenn Harrell, Peabody and George Pyle, Bobby Wicks and Joe Grant all standing on the bank, poised to dive into three feet of water.

A trip to Dripping Springs was always a lot of fun. There was competition to see who could get in the water first. There were no prizes to be won by the winner, of course, just bragging rights for the day. Most of the time a group of us would ride our bicycles down the long hill to the swimming hole.

On one occasion Freddy Beard was riding on the bike with me, sitting in the basket on the handlebars. I rolled right up to the edge of the hole, and Freddy dived into the waist deep water. We had won the competition for the day. Bobby Wicks, riding on the handlebars of Peabody's bicycle, then followed Freddy's dive in a matter of seconds...with nothing on that is, except his new Bulova watch given to him as a birthday present from his sister, Roberta. Needless to say, that was long before waterproof watches.

Occasionally when we were in swimming, a car would come down the hill and cross the bridge next to the swimming hole. Everybody would go under water until the car had gone out of sight. But there was a time when a carload of girls played hooky from school and drove down to the springs.

We spotted the car before they got there, and we all hid underwater again. A few seconds later we came up, but they were still there standing in front of the car! There we stood, waist deep in the water wearing nothing but our skin. They threatened to stay all day unless we got out of the water. After what seemed to be forever, the girls gave up and returned to the car, laughing as they went. At that point in our aquatic experience, we decided it was time to start wearing bathing suits.

CROFTON LAKE

Crofton Lake looked like the ocean to me when I was ten or eleven years old. It was quite mysterious and foreboding with shadows playing around the edge of the water. Today, people like to build houses near the lake or ocean. I don't remember any houses near the lake at that time. One of my friends once said that Crofton Lake looked like a place where people could drown.

That's exactly what happened to my cousin. Nadine Hammonds drowned in the lake at the age of thirteen. Her body was taken to the hospital, and the doctor said she had water in her lungs.

I guess as a result of that, I never really liked swimming there. In fact, I almost drowned there just a few years after Nadine's death.

Some of my friends and I had gone to the lake one afternoon. The sun was bright and hot, and the water was still. We untied an old boat we found at the edge of the water and got into it, four or five of us. We started to row across the lake to the other side. Somewhere along the way, we were diving off the boat and turned it upside down. The bathing suit I had borrowed had metal eyelets on the belt, and one accidentally slipped over a hook on the side of the boat. I was fastened to the boat, and I couldn't get free.

As the guys were turning the boat over, I was turning with it. I held my hand up out of the water, but they thought I was just playing. The water was beginning to choke me, and I found it hard to breathe. Presently, they saw I was in trouble and was able to right the boat and free me. That was one scary experience. I don't know whether they thought about it, but they really saved my life.

There were other misadventures at the lake too. Charley Barnes told me that he and Bobby Wicks were swimming at the lake once. They had taken off their watches and left them in their pockets on the bank. Bobby had a Bulova and Charley had an Elgin. When they got back to their clothes, Charley's watch was gone and Bobby's was still in his pocket. The watch was never found.

In the mid fifties Crofton Lake was a great place to park with your date. It was quite and dark and secluded. Rumors began floating around that couples were being stalked at the lake. Some guys got together, with one dressed as a girl, and parked their car near the water. They tried this several times, but no stalker was ever spotted. Some couples decided not to take a chance and stopped parking there.

A few years ago when I was visiting Crofton, my nephew, Larry Richardson, and I drove down the road toward the lake. I kept looking for it, but I could not find the lake. It was not there. In fact, it was difficult to picture where it was years ago. I'm sure Crofton Lake holds fonder memories for many, unlike the ones I have described here.

THE BLUFFS

It was fun to go to the bluffs when I was a kid. Generally, four or five of us would camp out at the bluffs often sleeping on the ground. You could hear all kinds of sounds after dark. We learned to identify all kinds of birds and animals and insects. It was fun cooking and eating our meals outside.

First, we would clean off a space to start a fire. Our meals were usually made up of hot dogs with all the trimmings and baked potatoes. Today's popular TV series "Survivor" reminds me of the time we spent on the bluffs together. Camping and playing in the woods was just a part of our activities.

We pooled our talents to earn spending money. Peabody was our resident scientist or botanist. He enjoyed the outdoors as a kid and still does today. He had a special talent of identifying trees in the winter, which we would mark, and come back and dig them up after the spring season. May Apple roots were plentiful. We would dig them up and sell them to Ben and Frank Gordon, who owned the mercantile stores. The roots would bring about five cents a pound. A more expensive root was ginseng, but more difficult to harvest. This plant would net about fifteen cents a pound.

Peabody was our point man, to find and identify these plants. George Pyle was our financial consultant, and chief negotiator in selling the products. George was a born salesman; he still is today. If harvesting a certain plant or catching a certain animal was dangerous, Glenn Harrell was our risk taker.

Glenn wasn't afraid of anything. He would wade into weeds waist high, where it was impossible to see your feet, to get berries and tell us where the snakes were. Once, he and I were sent out by our mothers to pick a gallon of blackberries. It took us quite a long time because we ate the berries about as fast as we picked them. Finally, the time came for us to go back home. My bucket was filled to the brim.

Glenn had a little more than half a bucket full, so he poured the berries out on the ground, filled the bucket half full of rocks and acorns and put his berries on top. The bucket looked full, but of course it was only half full. I told him that his mother would surely give him a whipping, but he only laughed and took them home.

When we arrived at his house, his mother was glad to see he had picked a gallon of berries. But when she poured them out to wash them, she discovered the hoax. I stood by and laughed as hard as I could while she whipped him all the way into the house.

The bluffs became a learning lab for all of us. Many of the lessons we learned are still being used today. Our favorite sport at the bluffs was climbing young trees and riding them to the ground. We learned by trial and error which trees were easiest and safest to climb and ride down. The sycamore tree was too brittle and likely to break, leaving you hanging too high off the ground. Little hickory saplings were the best and easiest to ride down. The trick was to climb up the tree as far as you could, and when it started to lean over you wanted to drop your full weight and enjoy a thrilling ride to the ground.

It is good that our parents were never aware of the risks we were taking. Had they known what we were doing; it might have shortened their lives. My mother never knew I was swimming. She used to tell me never to go in the water until I learned to swim, and never climb to the top of a tree.

PUNCH'S POOL ROOM

Most of the boys in Crofton grew up playing pool at Punch Croft's pool room. Punch ran a tight ship. He was a really nice person, but he wouldn't allow any rough-housing or bad language in his place of business. He knew there were a lot of kids who came there to play pool, and he wanted them to grow up in a clean environment. If anyone got into a fight or scuffle, they were asked to leave. Kids learned how to play pool, and they learned how to get along with others too. Where else could you go, be with nice people and really enjoy a good sport for ten cents a game?

There were a lot of good pool players in Crofton. Bill Barnett used to come to the pool room bringing his pool cue in a long round leather case. It was very impressive to the younger bunch to watch him take out the pool stick, put it together and break the pool balls.

Nine-ball was the game of choice for the better, betting, pool players. Reverend Gene Hellstern, pastor of the Christian Church for a number of years, would come and play pool every now and then. Some of our church members didn't really approve of that, but he sure brought a lot of young people into our church through that contact. He was a great role model for all of us too, but really wasn't a great pool shot.

Robert Renshaw, who graduated from high school in the class with many of the people mentioned in this book, was one of the best pool players in town. He was really smooth and knew the game. He earned the nickname "Instructor" because of his teaching ability, whether or not the advice was solicited.

Charlie Barnes and I played one particular game in a hurry. We had started a game of bank pool fifteen minutes before we were supposed to get on the bus to go out of town for a basketball game. We finished the game in three minutes. We won the basketball game that night too. Many a night, Punch had to run us out so he could close up and go home to supper.

Years later when I was a student at Vanderbilt Divinity School, I taught those Tennessee boys the Crofton way of playing pool. There was a billiard table in the Commons Room at Vandy. I'm sure we often spent more time at the table than we could afford. Billiards is not my game these days. I play golf in a foursome two or three days a week. When I make a bigger score than I should, I often say I'm giving up golf and taking up playing pool again.

CROFTON SCHOOL

The first schools in Crofton were privately owned and operated. The first Crofton public school was built in 1904 for grade school. The first high school graduation class was conducted at the end of the 1917-1918 school term with a whopping five graduates! Those receiving a diploma were: Logan McCord, J.F. Maddox, Mary Burkholder, Flossie Dukes and Beatrice Martin. On the other end of the school's history, the last graduating class was celebrated on May 25, 1959, with nineteen students receiving diplomas.

Crofton High School: 1951

This doesn't show much growth between five and nineteen graduates. Fire destroyed Crofton School three times between 1924 and 1951. The Crofton Common School's building was the first to burn down. After this tragedy Crofton became an independent system, and fire burned down the two-story brick building. Crofton School then merged into Christian County School system in 1948.

In 1951 it was again destroyed by fire. The fire occurred during the basketball season and practice was held at Lacy High School. The High School graduation exercises were held that year on the baseball field on our own baseball field.

Three or four of my friends, and I were driving home from Hopkinsville the night the school burned. We could see the red glare of the flames before we reached the city limits. We wondered where the fire was. Someone jokingly said he hoped it was the school building. The laughter soon turned into tears when we discovered our school building lay in ruins. The floors had been oil treated, meaning that not only did they make the soles of your shoes black as soot; they also caused the flames to explode like a tinderbox.

At that moment we could not imagine how our lives would be impacted. We must have stayed up all night sharing memories of our twelve years together in that building. Even now, fifty-five years after that tragedy, the school becomes the source of most of our recollections.

One of the highlights that we experience every three years is the School Reunion that brings us together again in the summer. The reunion is held not only for the class of 1951, but for every class since the school's birth. We have all exchanged many theories, opinions, and "being down right sure" about just how the fire occurred. Most of us have our own beliefs about it, and why it happened, but I guess we'll never know the facts about what happened that night in 1951. If we knew, someone could write a great mystery novel. I'll leave that to famous people who write books for a living.

After the Fire-Crofton High School: 1951

THE EAT SHOP

The Eat Shop was one of the busiest places in Crofton. I'm not sure about the date that the restaurant was opened. It was probably before World War II. At any rate I would venture a guess that nearly every person born in Crofton spent some time there. The food was excellent, and the service was top notch. Paul Jones told me that Babe Goodaker owned the Eat Shop for many years.

The restaurant served many functions in our fair city. It was not just another restaurant or cafe that sold food. It provided a place for the interchange of ideas. It was a civic center where politics were discussed, a gathering place for whatever you had planned.

The Eat Shop was a social center where many romances were begun, and possibly where some ended. It was generally a happy place. There was always a lot of laughter and camaraderie. It was a place where jokes were shared and stories swapped and friendships begun.

Then there was the indisputable "punch board" on the counter next to the cash register. For the novices among you, a punch board was made up of several little squares. Behind each square there was a number indicating how much you had to pay if you punched out that number. The cost ran from five cents, maybe up to fifty cents. When all the squares were punched out you could go for the prize behind the remaining big square. Quite often, a group of people would gather round and punch out all the squares just to see who would win the prize. It was a lot of fun, and it didn't cost very much.

I'm satisfied that hundreds of stories could be told about things that happened at the Eat Shop over the years. One such story involves James Ooley Price, and that was his real name. Ooley rode an old Indian motorcycle that had a gear shift on the left side. One night, a bunch of us were standing out in front of the Eat Shop when Ooley came roaring in and the cycle got away from him in the loose gravel. When the dust cleared and Ooley got to his feet, a part his ear lay in the gravel and maybe a tooth as well. It didn't seem to phase him, as he lifted the motorcycle, got on and rode away.

George Pyle tells of the time when he was hitch-hiking close to the Little River Bridge in Hopkinsville, also called "Hoptown." Ooley came along on that Indian motorcycle, picked George up, and made it to the Eat Shop twelve miles away in seven minutes. Needless to say, George went inside to use the restroom.

In writing this piece, I remember that Lev Gamble owned the restaurant once, too. I didn't want to leave that out. Pearl Barnes was probably working there at that time, since she worked there from the time I was old enough to buy a hamburger. She was the mother of Beaky Barnes, formally known as Charles Templeton Barnes. She was a great cook, fun to be around and probably knew every young person in Crofton.

There was always a crowd in the restaurant on weekends. If any serious customers had come in for a hamburger, I don't know where they would have found a seat. Many of us sitting around were buying customers some of the time and just loafers part of the time. That didn't seem to make any difference to the management. There was no place like the Eat Shop in town just to hang out. Lev would be cook up the hamburgers in a big old iron skillet and when the burgers were done, there would be a pint of grease left. Your guess is as good as mine as to what happened to the grease.

A part of the fun was to slip the salt and pepper shakers into someone's coat pocket as they sat around eating and talking. Often they would get all the way home before they found them and would have to bring them back.

Kids were always thinking up things to do to make a little money. One way to make some quick cash was to get a dime from all the participants and put the money in a hat. As cars came down the highway, we would see who could run across the highway closest to the car coming head on. The winner collected all the dimes. It seems that Gilbert Harrell was the frequent winner. He was fast, and would run across the road so close to the car that he could touch the front bumper. Of course, the driver of the car would often run off the highway, scared half to death. There must have been a full time angel lurking around the Eat Shop to protect crazy kids like us.

Yes, the Eat Shop in Crofton was surely one of the Seven Wonders of our little world. A place where history was made and memories will linger is now occupied by a dollar store. The Eat Shop is no more.....except in our memory.

The Eat Shop

THE PLAY PARK

Long before the completion of beautiful Gordon Park honoring Ben and Tilly Gordon, there was Play Park. This park was created primarily by five boys: Glenn Harrell, Peabody, George Pyle, Joe Grant and myself. All five of us lived in the area where the park was built. The five of us planned it and built it with our own hands, and it served many kids in the neighborhood.

The park was designed and built in a vacant area between my house and Joe Grant's house. It was a grassy area that included a small pond and many tall broadleaf trees. Grass was scraped off an area for basketball. We built a flying jenny. A small tree was cut down and a hole bored in the stump with a long board attached loosely by a large bolt. Two persons could ride, one sitting on each end of the board. The board was spun round and round. When you got off the flying jenny you would stagger all over the place.

A favorite game was "dare base". A group was divided into two teams of an equal number of players. The players formed a line several yards apart. One team would send a player as close to the other team's line as possible. Then that player would be chased back to his or her base. If the player who gave the "dare" was tagged, that person had to become a member of the opposing team. The team with the most members at the end of the game was declared a winner. "Red Rover" was another favorite.

The small pond in the park area provided a place to fish or to go "frog giggin." Some times we would just shoot at the frogs with our sling shots. Joe Grant was an expert marksman with the sling shot. If he had lived in Old Testament times, he would have replaced David in the slaying of the giant Goliath. The rest of us were just novices compared to Joe.

A lot of time was devoted to finding just the right size pebbles and rocks to use for ammunition. One summer the road that ran by Herbert Williams house was newly graveled. We would walk out that road, maybe a quarter of a mile, and fill our pockets to overflowing with choice pebbles. Such painstaking efforts would last us maybe two days, and then we would search for more stones.

More important than the right size pebbles was the selection of a sling shot. Weeks could be spent in the search for the right kind of wood from which to whittle out a prize sling shot. Just as people today carry their cell phones with them wherever they go, we had our sling shots on us at all times. Well, maybe not at all times; I guess we didn't take them to Sunday school and church. The type wood, size, and color of the sling shot was part of our personae.

This is my opinion, of course, but I always felt that hickory trees offered the best wood. The hickory is a tough, pale wood, and easy to whittle. An inner tube from an old tire provided the rubber bands to propel the pebbles with strength and accuracy. A foray into dad's closet to cut the tongue out of one of his shoes gave us the launching pad for this invincible weapon. A strong shoe string or a thin wire could attach the rubber bands and pads on to the stock. We were then in business, and the hunt began.

Between the ages of eight and sixteen, a bicycle is a necessity. That was the primary mode of transportation, sitting astride your green, floating-on-air, Schwinn bicycle...with a horn on the fuselage, headlights on the front fender and luggage rack on the back. A sling shot in your back pocket and chewing on a Milky Way candy bar....it didn't get any better than that!

There was another vehicle of sorts that was a stand-by that went everywhere you were walking. It was an apparatus that brought symmetry and form to each step you took. It was actually a wheel that measured twelve to fifteen inches in diameter. A long coat hanger with a kink at one end could be placed against the edge of the wheel that would push it along at the speed you were walking. If your mother sent you to the grocery store to get a loaf of bread, it was suave to push your wheel along. It was just something to do but, hey, for an eight or nine year old it was cool.

The thing about it is, kids in those days were more inventive than most kids today. We had to be inventive because most of us had few toys. We made our own toys, created our own games and designed our own inventions.

(L-R): George and Eldon Pyle

A TYPICAL SUNDAY IN CROFTON

Following a breakfast of scrambled eggs, country ham, red-eye gravy, biscuits made from scratch with sorghum molasses, coffee and milk, it was time to get ready for Sunday school and church. In our early years most of us went without our parents. My mother would always give me a nickel or dime for my offering.

After church, we usually went back home to change clothes and hitch-hike to Hoptown, where we would go to the Alhambra Theater for the two o'clock movie. This was our regular ritual. It was customary to go to Ferrell's to eat lunch before the movie. Most of the time I would order two cheeseburgers, a coke, and a slice of New York Strawberry Creme pie, all for about forty cents.

Tickets for the movie cost ten to fifteen cents if you were under age twelve. Some of us were twelve for about three years. The Alhambra was the most beautiful theater in Hoptown. They don't build theaters like that any more. The inside was really plush, with a thick carpet on the floor and three or four sets of curtains on the stage. When the lights dimmed and one curtain was drawn, there was usually a comedy or a serial before the main feature. We were sometimes late for that due to the long line for popcorn and cokes. Another curtain would then open for commercials. With the opening of the third curtain, the movie began. The opening of all those curtains and the music was really exciting.

It was at the Alhambra that I saw my first 3-D movie. Three-colored glasses were handed out as we entered the theater. These 3-D glasses caused the action on the screen to appear to come right out into the audience. If there was a scene where someone threw a chair at somebody else, it looked like it was coming right at you.

Films in Technicolor were shown in the late forties or the early fifties. That was really something, moving from the black and white pictures. When the movie was over, there were usually three or more of us who would walk out to the edge of town and hitch-hike back home. Back in those days it was pretty easy to catch a ride. There was never a thought that we might get into a car with criminals and be kidnapped or hurt. Many times we were lucky enough to hitch a ride with someone we knew.

Suppertime was usually around five-thirty. We would eat at home again and then turn right around and hitch-hike back to Hoptown to go to the seven o'clock movie at the Princess Theater. The Princess wasn't quite as upscale as the Alhambra, but it gave us a chance to see another movie we hadn't viewed before. Every once in a while, we would see a film at the Kentucky Theater across the street from the Princess. We didn't go there often because the theater was dirty looking, and some said when the lights dimmed the rats would come and eat popcorn out of your sack. Of course, after the movie we would go back to Ferrell's to eat more hamburgers before we began hitch-hiking home. Two movies and two meals, all in one day for under a dollar, weren't half bad.

(L-R) Top: Bill Hammonds, Eldon Pyle
Bottom :Charlie Barnes, Bobby Wicks

    Terry Capps told me once about an experience he had trying to catch a ride home after dark. He said he and one of the Manasco brothers left the nine o' clock movie in Hoptown and walked out to the edge of town to catch a ride. After standing in one place an hour or so, they started walking and sticking out their thumb at each passing car. They soon realized they might not catch a ride at all, but they kept on walking.

He arrived at his house in Crofton about an hour before daylight. He said he remembered his bedroom window was unlocked, so he climbed in the window and went to bed in his clothes. Terry said he felt like he had been asleep about ten minutes when his mother came into his bedroom and told him to get up and get ready for school. Thankfully, he arrived home safely that night. But the twelve mile hike left him with awfully sore feet. In case that happened again, he said he always had enough change to ride the Greyhound bus.

SCHOOL DAZE

The seventh and eighth grade classes during the years 1945-50 were taught in the same room, upstairs in the old school building. The two grades were divided by a center aisle that ran the length of the classroom. There must have been at least thirty students enrolled. I was in the seventh grade when I entered this hall of horrors. Some of the eighth graders looked to be seventeen or eighteen years of age. This mixed group of misfits ran off about seven teachers in one year.

As I remember the loudest, most difficult-to-control students were seated at the back of the room. This proved to be a grave mistake for students and teacher alike. For one thing, students on the back row were difficult for the teacher to see. Some of the boys had small sling-shots made from clothes hangers from which they could launch projectiles at students near the front of the room. Eventually, a full blown war broke out between the classes.

There were some unspoken rules to which the more savvy students subscribed. If the teacher had to leave the room for some reason, some of the older inmates would antagonize the younger ones. Of course, no one dared tell the teacher what had happened. If someone gave the name of one of the perpetrators to the teacher, the snitch was mauled at recess. Very few students squealed on each other.

W. W. Chumbler was both principal and basketball coach at this time. He not only held these two offices but was chief executor of punishment. Any student apprehended breaking a rule, written or unwritten, would get a first class paddling and hair-pulling. "W. W.", as he was affectionately called, was about five-feet tall and weighed in about two-fifty.

During the uprisings in the seventh and eighth grades, he would occasionally try to slip up the stairs to the classroom and catch someone misbehaving. Of course, you could hear his footsteps long before he got to the second landing. He also had about two dozen keys dangling from his belt, and you could hear them jingling long before he peeked around the door. Naturally, he was unsuccessful in every attempt. These were hard-core, well trained students he was up against.

Some of these students in the eighth grade had keen, criminal minds that would have made John Dillinger look like a kindergarten teacher. Looking back on my time in that class, it makes me wonder if I couldn't have missed that experience and come out better. Anyway, it leaves me with some exciting memories in my old age.

TEACHERS REMEMBERED

Two of the greatest basketball coaches at Crofton High School were Milton Traylor and William Lile. I was not on the basketball team when Traylor coached, but only when Lile coached. He just may have a few four letter words for me. There were many fine players that played on the Crofton Cougars team to compliment these two great coaches.

I can remember some excellent teachers at Crofton during my twelve years of schooling. Miss Louise Tweddell got her students started off on the right foot in the first grade. What a sweet person she was! She was a teacher, mother and mentor all rolled into one. She was a caring soul who dearly loved children. Not only did her students love her, but the parents loved her as well.

All the parents of six-year olds wanted their children in Miss Louise's room. If you came to school a little unkempt with dirt on your hands or face, she would quietly take you to the back of the room and wash the dirt off, and then give you a big hug. I don't remember how long she taught first grade, but she taught it long enough to touch hundreds of children and their parents.

Miss Charlie Ledford taught geography in high school. I think she came to Crofton from South Christian. She was a robust woman who limped around with a frown on her face occasionally. I think her feet must have hurt her, or perhaps her shoes didn't fit well. She was a great teacher, strict and fair. She felt her students ought to be serious in the classroom. The junior and senior classes must have tried her patience.

Perhaps you've read somewhere that prison inmates often tried to make weapons to escape. Well, it seemed like some students were guilty of the same thing. I can recall a popular little invention in the class room in those days. It was made from a bobby pin, and when straightened out and connected to a school desk, could make a lot of noise. You could take your finger and twang it a bit ,and it would vibrate for a few seconds in a loud noise.

I believe that Freddy Beard must have been the inventor of such a toy. At least, he was a master at twanging the little device and remaining undetected. This little noise drove Miss Charlie to distraction. She would hobble around the room and ask who made the noise. She always suspected Freddy whether he was guilty or not. Miss Charlie eventually moved to Hoptown to teach. She taught us well and touched our lives for the better.

Gwendolyn Wilkins taught English in my senior year. She also served as chaperone for our senior trip to New Orleans. Gwendolyn was an excellent teacher, a good sport, and made learning fun. The English Literature class was one of my favorites. Our English class was in the new building after the old school burned. There was a sink at the back of the room. The room may have been used as a Chemistry class one time. I can remember a large plant on the counter near the sink. Carl Taylor was always experimenting with various liquids to get the plant to grow. Of course, Mrs. Wilkins didn't know this. I have to tell you that at the end of our senior year that plant was five feet tall! You'll have to ask Taylor what he did to get the plant to finally grow.

During our senior year we were told we had to memorize the poem "Thanatopsis," by William Cullen Bryant, to be able to graduate. To the best of my memory every student stood and recited the poem, except Elbert Rhodes. Elbert was a master at solving math problems, but he couldn't memorize "Mary Had A Little Lamb". He attempted to recite the poem on several occasions. Finally, the final day came to stand and recite the verses. I sat in front of him and held the book of poetry open on my desk so that he could see every word. He choked a few times, but received a passing grade. Thankfully, I was not implicated in the ruse.

W.W. Chumbler was principal and coach for two or three years at Crofton. It was unknown whether he had ever coached or not. However, he was a tyrant at training. The Cougars may not have won every game they played, but they were probably the best conditioned team in the state. W.W. was very nervous during a game. He would sweat profusely and bite his nails constantly. Whenever you were pulled out of a game you had to sit-down by him on the bench. None of us liked that because he would put his hot, sweaty arm around your shoulder while he was talking to you.

Our practice sessions five days a week would last about an hour or an hour and a half. At the end of the practice, we had to duck walk around the gym and run twenty or more laps. Then all the players would line up and he would make each of us drink down a large spoonful of cod liver oil, out of the same spoon.

There were so many good teachers at Crofton from whom we received a fine education: Aileen Nichols, Jack Speegle, Ila Marie Hight, Melvie Hurd, T.H. Likens and many, many more. They filled an important role for those of us who became a CHS graduate.

1951 Senior Trip to New Orleans

(L-R) Back Row: Bobby Wicks; Dottie Knight; Margie Bone; Wilma Thompson; Ovaline Pennington; Marjorie Johnson; Beth Cansler; Glenda Hayes; Nancy Clark; Gwendolyn Wilkins; Bobby Cavanaugh; Juanita Young; Bill Hammonds

Front Row: Eldon Pyle; Robert Renshaw

WILD WEEK-END ESCAPADES
PART I

One weekend Bobby Wicks, Charlie Barnes and I made a trip to Union City, Tennessee. Barely out of Hoptown, Bobby announced that our car had no brakes. This revelation was news we didn't want to hear. He assured us not to worry, but here we were, starting out on a hundred mile trip with no brakes. We arrived safely in Union City about eleven o'clock that night, and spent the rest of it in a motel.

The next morning we picked up the girls we went to spend the day with, Chris Reddick, Betty Fox and Foncene King. We drove to Reel Foot Lake, where we must have seen a dozen or more eagles while we swam and had a picnic lunch. Late that evening we took the girls home, and the next morning we headed back to Crofton.

Bobby got sleepy, and asked me if I wanted to drive. I took over as driver, but a few miles down the road we got behind an old lady driving about ten miles an hour. As we approached a crossroad, and the old lady stuck her left hand out the window indicating she was going to make a left turn. Since our car didn't have any brakes, I just veered to the right in order to keep from gearing down. Just as I made this maneuver, the woman made the prettiest right turn you've ever seen. Our car ricocheted off of hers.

I eventually geared the car down to a stop, and we jumped out and ran over to see if the woman was hurt. She was outside her car looking at the right front fender. An old man who had been sitting on his front porch walked over, and said he had witnessed the whole thing. It was the woman's fault, he said. She had given a left signal and turned right into our car. There was just a tiny scratch on her fender, so she said for us to just go on home, and she would get it repaired. We apologized, and ran back to our car as fast as we could.

Bobby was wide-awake by now, and hopped in the driver's seat, but in his anxiety he backed into an old parked car. The old man who had witnessed everything came off the porch slowly, and without saying a word, looked his car over shaking his head. There was a slight dent in his front bumper. Bobby asked how much he thought it would cost to repair the dent. The old man thought for a moment, and said, 'I reckon it would take about two dollars." Hurriedly we handed him two one dollar bills, and jumped back into our car, tires squealing as we got back on the highway.

Here, we had been involved in two separate car wrecks in less than fifteen minutes, and without getting involved with the police or paying for any damages. No one was hurt, and the scratches on Bobby's old '37 Ford could be simonized out quite easily. We figured an angel must have been watching over us.

WILD WEEK-END ESCAPADES
PART II

Few of the people mentioned in this book had a car or truck of their own during the time period mentioned. A few, however, did have access to a vehicle occasionally. Every now and then, usually in the summer, Jackie Myers used to come to Crofton to visit his grandparents, Ernest and Lucy Myers. Mr. Myers was a funeral director and, of course, owned a hearse. Jackie and I would push the old Packard hearse out of the garage and away from his grandparents' house to a spot where we could safely start it without being heard. We would pack as many as six or seven in the back of the hearse and head for the drive-in movie in Hoptown.

Jackie would drive and one other person would sit in the front seat with him. The rest would lie down in the back under a blanket. Jackie would buy two tickets for the drive-in movie and park next to a speaker. The speaker was hung on the front window so all of us could hear the movie. One of the crew would usually get out of the hearse and go to the concession stand and order popcorn and cokes for all of us. To this day I don't even like to think what would have happened if his grandfather woke up during the night and looked for his hearse.

ADVENTURES IN DRIVING

If it isn't obvious by now, while I was growing up in Crofton, not many teenagers had cars. We didn't need anybody to "pimp our ride" because we didn't own one. We were able to make friends with Bobby Wicks' brother, Ardell, who was a WWII veteran. He always had a sharp-looking car, and as an auto mechanic, he always kept it in top shape. He was extremely particular about it though, and didn't want anything spilled in the car or anything torn.

Much of the time Ardell, Bobby, George, Peabody, Charlie Barnes and I would ride to Hoptown for homemade ice cream at Tongate's drive-in restaurant. Tongate's had pretty girl hops, who would come out to your car and take food orders. Since Ardell always had more money than the rest of us, he would tip the car hop. Sometimes, he would roll up a one dollar bill and drop it inside an empty coke bottle. I'm sure the girl never really got a rush out of this, but we always got a laugh out of it.

We once figured that Ardell drove us at least a thousand miles over a two year period. He always bought the gasoline, back when it was only fifteen cents or so a gallon. You could practically fill up your car for two dollars. Ardell was nearly seven years older than any of us, but that didn't seem to matter. We always had fun together.

One Friday night, all of us met at the Eat Shop to make a trip to Hoptown. Ardell showed us the new Indian blanket he had bought to cover the rear seat, to protect it against Coke spills and the like. He told us to be careful, and not to tear the blanket. Well, we got back from the Eat Shop about ten-thirty that night, and George had lit up a cigarette just before we arrived. As we were getting out of the car, the blanket caught on fire. Ardell pulled it out, but not before the fire left a large hole right in the center of the blanket. Despite the fire, the evening had been fun and even Ardell laughed with the rest of us. Instead of Butch Cassidy's "hole-in-the-wall gang," we thought of ourselves as the "hole-in-the-blanket gang." Ardell assured us he would buy another blanket.

For none of us to have owned a car, we sure were on the road a lot. One day, we were taking the scenic trip to Dripping Springs in an old 40's model car owned by Mike Dulin. We called him Junior, and he worked in the strip mines and drove a gob truck five days a week. This was a pleasure trip on Saturday morning with about six or seven of us in the car. I was on the driver's side running board, and George was on the passenger's side board.

Junior was driving pretty fast, as he always did, but he knew the road as well as he knew the back of his hand. What he didn't know that day was that the bridge was out, leaving a wide ditch right in the middle of the road. George and I saw the dilemma about the same time and screamed out that the bridge was gone. Mike started gearing the old car down to maintain better control, and it was clear that he planned to ride it out.

George and I decided it was best for us to jump off the running boards, figuring we would not come out very well when the car hit the hole. Fortunately, none of us were injured, although the car took quite a jolt and had to be repaired. George said that when he got home, and his mother saw the look on his face, she asked "Well, you've been in a wreck, haven't you?" He never figured out how she knew, but instead chalked it up to a mother's intuition.

That wreck reminds me of an email I received, in which a fellow was talking about the death of his grandfather. He said that when he died, he wanted to go like his grandfather did…with a smile on his face. He didn't want to go screaming at the top of his lungs like the others in the car when his grandfather ran through a stop sign, hitting an eighteen wheeler at seventy-five miles an hour.

There were a lot of wild drivers in Crofton, with whom we trusted our lives. If NASCAR had become a national sport then, many of them would have qualified as drivers beating out Jeff Gordon or Kurt Busch for a title. Ooley Price, Mike Dulin and John Cornelius were the most infamous…but John was a speed demon. He walked fast, ate fast, talked fast, and drove his Plymouth convertible fast. One day, I made the mistake of riding with him to Hoptown and back. He peeled rubber out of the Eat Shop parking lot and headed down the road as fast as he could. He drove all the way to Hoptown at eighty miles an hour. We spent only about half an hour there, and started back to Crofton.

We were following several cars on a curve around Billy Goat Inn at about thirty miles an hour when John grew restless. He said, "I'm counting to three, and then I'm going to pass all five of those cars." I hadn't done much praying at my age, but in a split second I graduated from amateur status to a professional. John stomped the accelerator to the floorboard and began passing. We passed all five of them and just made it back into our lane in time to miss hitting a pickup truck head-on. I never rode with John again. Thank you, Lord!

Some Sissies Taking Shots
(L-R): Charlie Barnes, George Pyle, Billy Wagoner

AN ERSTWHILE DATING EXPERIMENT

Howard "Pieface" Lloyd and I had known each other for some time. Pieface went to school in Nortonville and I went to school in Crofton. We became friends when he worked at the DX Station and I was employed at Randall's Ice House. Two things caused us to form an alliance. Pieface had an automobile. I had been able to arrange a date for us with two blonde nursing students who worked at Jennie Stuart Hospital.

Our date with these girls was set for the following Saturday night in Hoptown. We were to meet them at the hospital and go out for dinner and a movie. The die had been cast; we had a week to whip ourselves into shape. We would get together very soon to plan our strategy.

A friend of mine told me the girls were a year or two older than Pieface and I. Pieface was eighteen and I was seventeen. The girls were nineteen and twenty-one. The first stage of our plan was to make ourselves seem older than we actually were. I suggested we pass ourselves off as two college students. Since we were both still in high school, we had to figure out where we were enrolled in college. We both had school sweaters. His sweater had a large letter "N" on it. Mine had a bright orange letter "C".

Pieface quickly decided he would be from Notre Dame. That sounded ok to me. Suddenly I thought of a small college I had read about in central Kentucky - Centre College. That would explain the letter "C" on my sweater. Our only hope was that neither of our dates had ever seen a sweater from either of these colleges.

The next Saturday evening at seven o'clock, two pretend college students arrived at Jennie Stuart Hospital to meet Sara and Dottie, our dates. We took them to Tongate's Drive-in Restaurant and then on to the Alhambra Theater. For some unexplained reason, the dating experiment didn't work out too well for either of us that night. We never tried again.

ANOTHER DATING EXPERIMENT GONE AWRY

There was another occasion between the sexes where things didn't go as planned. I had been out of high school about a month and was dating a girl in Hoptown. She told me she had a girlfriend that needed a date for the next Friday night. The name of a close friend immediately came to mind…Billy Wagoner.

I called Billy the next night and asked if he would like to date a friend of my girlfriend's on Friday night. Of course, he wanted to know something about this girl. What did she look like? How old was she? Was she a lot of fun? Where would we go on this date? Well, since I had never seen this girl myself, I could hardly answer any of his questions. I finally persuaded him that she was pretty, had a good personality and was a lot of fun. He said he would go.

A day or two before the date, Billy and I had lunch at Ferrell's. I was kidding him, and I told him his date weighed about 160 pounds, was four feet and six inches tall and had a speech impediment. We both laughed. Friday evening arrived. Billy got out of the car and walked up to the house with my girlfriend. What I'm about to tell you is the honest truth. This girl looked exactly like I had described her. When he got in the back seat with this girl, all the color had drained out of his face. He was silent as we made our way to the movie.

I thought he would probably kill me after we dropped off our dates and started back to Crofton. Being a good friend, he laughed it off. But to this day, he refuses to believe that I had never laid eyes on the girl before. He was very cautious about double dating after that.

Heavy Weight Match: Billy Wagoner vs. Bill Hammonds
April 1954

BASKETBALL TRIVIA: CROFTON COUGARS

Undoubtedly there are many basketball stories in the annals of the Crofton Cougars, about players and games. Some of the best stories come from road trips when the Cougars played away from home. Our basketball team over the years was made up of many colorful and outstanding players.

Wilford Grace was such a player that comes to mind. He played at the position of guard. He was a good ball handler and often a showman on the floor. He chewed gum as he dribbled the ball up and down the court. One night in a game at Sinking Fork High School, he was blowing bubbles as he dribbled the ball. Somehow a Sinking Fork player took the ball away from him. Well, this didn't impress our coach, W.W., so he sat Wilford on the bench.

The coach sent me into the game as point guard. I was playing well that night and made three set shots in a row. Wilford never started another game. I played that spot for a long time. Wilford worked in Chicago one summer and came back to school with a new hair style. His hair was piled up on his head six inches high. He was really a character and was well liked by everyone.

Carl Taylor was another outstanding player, a left handed ball-handler. He had a fast dribble that was nearly unstoppable. When he dribbled the ball down the floor his tennis shoes made the whining sound of a truck tire. Taylor was recruited from the suburbs of Crofton in Mannington, Kentucky. He had played on the Nortonville team. He proved to be a real asset to our team. The deal was almost like stealing Michael Jordan from the Chicago Bulls. At the first of every game I tried to tap the ball to Taylor, knowing that he could beat everybody else down the floor and score the first two points.

Taylor was not only a good basketball player, but became a fine coach when he graduated from college. He coached high school teams for many years in Tennessee and Florida, and was a college basketball coach in Alabama. I see Taylor and his wife, Debra, every year when my family goes to Destin, Florida. We get together and eat and swap stories about the "old days".

One summer he told me the story about an away game in Dalton, Kentucky. The guest dressing room for players was a small room with a ten-foot ceiling that had one lone light bulb hanging from a wire. On this night a kid from Dalton was playing center. In Taylor's words, "He was the tallest, ugliest human I had ever seen." This kid was always pushing off and elbowing you under the basket. Once when he jumped and attempted to dunk the ball, Taylor caught the bottom of his shorts and jerked them down. The player responded by trying to elbow Taylor, but Taylor ducked and the guy's elbow hit Robert Renshaw in the eye, sending him to the bench. There were no bathroom facilities in our dressing room other than a five-gallon can sitting in one corner. Those were the days to remember.

Crofton Cougars 1949-1950 Basketball Team

(L-R) Back row: W.W. Chumbler; Gilbert Harrell; Elbert Rhodes; David Armstrong; Wilford Grace; Eldon Pyle; Bobby Wicks

Front Row: Russell Mitchell; Buddy Witherspoon; Delbert Rhodes; Howard Martin; Gene Hood; James Wells; Bill Hammonds

Peabody was a fine player, usually playing at the forward position. He was one of the highest jumpers on the team. He would dribble in to the basket with his legs folded up like the landing gear on a jet plane. Occasionally someone would foul him in that position and he would fall like a tree. He would get up and shake himself off and shoot two free throws. Peabody was fast, a good handler, and could be counted on to score consistently.

Elbert "Bulldog" Rhodes and Taylor played guard our senior year in school. They were two of the best ball players in the state. Bulldog earned his nickname by closely guarding his opponent. He would get on you like a "dog on a bone." He was not a high scorer, due to an eye ailment, but you could count on the player he guarded not scoring much either. Delbert, the brother of Bulldog, was also a fine player who graduated a year earlier. The Rhodes brothers died several years ago. If I'm not mistaken, Bulldog played on the first team in the eighth grade.

Rounding out the fifth position on the team were Freddy Beard and Robert Renshaw, alternating at the position of forward. They were both good players that you could count on in every game. George Pyle and Bobby Adams served as managers for a while, and they were the best. Back in those days basketballs were made out of leather. Our managers polished the basketballs for every game. They worked hard and were appreciated by the team.

JOBS AVAILABLE TO YOUNGSTERS FROM 1945-50

There were no Americorp jobs available. The Peace Corps had not come on the scene. A few years before World War II electrification had come to this part of the country. Now people could discard their old kerosene lamps and get rid of candles. Electric appliances were available to those who could afford them, but the town of Crofton had no running water. Even the old hotel got its water from a well. The barber shop had to transport water for shampooing and shaving. It was at this point that I made use of my entrepreneurship. Luckily, one of the barbers, T.M. Melton, was my uncle.

He contracted with me to haul water from the depot, just across the railroad from the shop. The means of transportation was a large zinc washtub. I called on some of my associates to help me once a week. It took 10 tubs of water to fill up the big tank behind the barber shop. We were paid the handsome sum of 10 cents a tub. I kept that franchise for about a year and then sought more lucrative employment.

One summer job I had was with the Kentucky Store and Land Company, affectionately called "The Company Store", by the coal miners and their families. This store was the main trading place for miners who wanted to charge their groceries and other supplies on credit a month at a time. The store's name reminds me of the lyrics of Tennessee Ford's song, "Sixteen Tons." It goes something like this:

> *You load sixteen tons, what do you get*
> *Another day older and deeper in debt*
> *Saint Peter don't you call me 'cause I can't go*
> *I owe my soul to the company store*

Well, my job was not shoveling coal, but my dad worked in the mines a number of years. My summer job was a "gofer", go for this and that, and get whatever was needed. There were groceries to be bagged or boxed and delivered. My main job at the close of each day's work was to clean up the meat saw. This high level job was usually given to the last hired person. Do you remember how fresh, sweet strawberries smell? Well, this odor was the opposite of that! It was an odor that was as stifling as a five pound rotten egg!

Every once in a while I would go with Paul Jones, a budding executive in the company, to deliver a truck load of supplies. Sometimes we would take a truck load to the tug boats at Uniontown, Kentucky. The tug boats pushed coal up and down the river. One route was to Alabama and another was up north somewhere. We would deliver groceries to families who didn't have transportation.

I can remember one such family made up of eight or ten children. They lived in an old house that had no screens on the windows. This didn't make much difference because in the summer the door was always left open anyway. The chickens and dogs and cats wandered in and out of the house at will. I can remember a teenage boy unloading the sacks of groceries. He would take out a carton of cigarettes and throw a pack to each of his younger brothers and sisters like it was a candy bar.

You could always find yard work. The going rate for lawns in those days was about a quarter for a small yard and maybe fifty cents for a half acre lawn. My best paying mowing job was for Ray Clark. He had a mid-size lawn and paid seventy-five cents. I think it was because he was one of my neighbors, and we attended the Crofton Christian Church where he was an elder.

I can remember one lawn I mowed where a large dog was tied to a clothes line. The rope had some sort of hook in it that allowed the dog to run the length of the yard. I really sweated a lot on that yard, trying to outrun the dog. All this work was done with a Sears and Roebuck push, rotary blade lawnmower.

Farm work was available during the summer and fall. There was hay to bail and put in the barn, tobacco to be set out, succored topped and cut and fired in the barn. Everybody raised a garden.

One of my lesser paying jobs was working in tobacco for Boyce Thomas. The rows of tobacco plants seemed a mile long.

Kids working in the tobacco patch for the first time were usually initiated by having to bite off the head of a huge, green, wiggly tobacco worm. I was about 14 years old when I worked for Mr. Thomas. He would pick up his workers at a designated place and drive them out to his farm. We would work from early in the morning until the sun set in the evening, and after the pigs were slopped. We ate lunch and supper at the farm and then Mr. Thomas would take us back to our homes. No one probably ever thought of child labor laws, and of course we were paid well, $1.25 for a day's work.

One of the more lucrative summer jobs I held was working at the Roy Randall's Ice House, adjacent to the DX Service Station. After I got my driver's license I drove a truck and delivered ice all over town. The ice came in large 300 pound blocks. They were loaded on the truck and wrapped in a tarp to slow the melting. You had to cut the ice with a pick into whatever size the customer wanted.

There was a diamond-shaped card placed in a window at the front of the house. The card was marked 100 pounds, 50 pounds, 25 pounds or 10 pounds. When you drove by a house you watched for signs that indicated how much ice the customer wanted that day. The ice was cut in the truck and carried by tongs into the house and placed in an ice box. The job paid well, $18.00 a week. Of course, there were no health benefits, no 401K's and no IRA's. I must admit though, at that salary, I started thinking about retirement.

WORKING CAN BE FUN

Throughout the school year, there were several events for community participation. Donkey basketball was one of the favorite events. For a nominal fee, participants could ride the donkeys that were there during the game. The game was played with similar rules, except that the trainers had the option to hit the donkeys with a shock stick anytime they chose. Just about the time a player rode his donkey under the goal for a lay-up, the trainers would shock the donkey and cause it to jump and buck the rider.

I saw Alfred Dyer riding a rather small donkey one night. Alfred was about six foot, five inches tall with legs dragging the floor. It looked funny because he was actually weighing the donkey down. The trainers would shock the animal, but Alfred would just keep riding it all the way under the basket to score. The game was a lot of fun, and the school always made a good profit.

W. W. Chumbler was not only our principal and coach, but an organizer par excellence. During our senior year, he came up with the idea of a "Duck Derby". Our players were sent out to ask the farmers to donate several ducks to run in the derby. Close to twenty ducks were in the race. Each duck had a card on his back with a number. The winning duck in each race received a small award. The cost for a ticket to the derby was probably a quarter.

Our basketball banquet was held later that year. The ducks had been killed and frozen before that. The meal served at the banquet was, you guessed it, duck and dressing. A charge was also made for the meal.

Another event that brought in a lot of people and a large profit for the school was square dancing. There would always be a fiddle player, and that is where I really learned to dance. The gym floor was spread with sawdust to minimize scratching, and bottled drinks and snacks were always plentiful.

Of course, after each event the sawdust had to be removed, the bottles and paper picked up and the trash carried out. Our principal, Chumbler, would usually appoint three or four boys to do this job, but before this cleanup actually happened, we usually had a lot of fun with it! We would play like we were commandoes on the front line, pick up the empty pop bottles and throw them like grenades at the brick wall. We would then fall on the sawdust floor to keep from getting shot by the enemy.

We probably broke twenty-five or thirty bottles every time we worked that job. Of course, all the glass had to be cleaned up with the sawdust, but we had a lot of fun while we were working.

PERSONALITIES

MISS LOUISE TWEDDELL, as I mentioned before, was a wonderful, much loved teacher. She had the face of an angel and a loving spirit to match. Miss Louise was loved and adored by every child she ever taught. Every parent wanted their children in her class.

In 1938 Miss Louise organized a band in her first grade class. I was chosen to play the snare drum. Each child's mother was responsible for sewing the band uniform. The material used was satin, with black pants and orange shirts, the school colors.

We were a proud bunch of first graders, as if we were in Tommy Dorsey's band. The band played on two or three occasions for the school during the year. During the following years, and even after we graduated from high school, whenever we met Miss Louise anywhere, she had to hug and kiss us with tears streaming down her face, and would want us to tell her what we were doing.

One of the great honors I received years later when I was a seminary student at Vanderbilt was being asked to preach her husband's funeral. Neither she nor I could have ever imagined that back when I was in her first grade class

POLY JONES was somewhat of an enigma. No one knew if Poly was his real name or not. He was a mystery of sorts. Few knew where he came from or where he lived, and knew nothing about his family. Poly would stop by the DX Service station frequently. He always wore two or three coats regardless of the temperature. When he came in, someone would ask, "How are you doing, Poly"? His answer was always, "Well, I guess I'm okay." Then someone would ask if he wanted a cold drink, and he would say, "It doesn't make any difference, anything is all right." Every time!

On one occasion, Poly said he was ordering a wife from a catalog. After that was announced, someone always asked if his wife had arrived. Finally, he told them her clothes had come and she would soon be there. Although the wife never came, he did order a complete sawmill C.O.D. Amazingly, it was shipped and unloaded at the Crofton Depot.

The one thing people remember Poly Jones for was his inexhaustible supply of "gogglin news." Kids would see Poly walking towards them and they would rush up to him and ask, "Do you have any gogglin news today"? He would dig down into one of his several pockets and come up with a scrap of paper. The gogglin news contained a language of its own: cat whiskers, dog eyebrows, chicken toenails, frog's teeth. We would always have fun reading the gogglin news even though we knew there was no intrinsic meaning or mystical reality about it.

To this day, I can picture Poly Jones shuffling his feet, dressed in several layers of clothing with a two or three day stubble, unkempt, making his way along the road with a knapsack on his shoulder. As I think back on the times I have seen him, I often wish someone had taken the time to really get to know him.

JIM DUNCAN operated a blacksmith shop in the middle forties and early fifties on Highway 41. As a boy, I found this an intriguing place to visit. Kids were always dropping by the shop to watch Mr. Duncan shoe horses and hammer out horseshoes. There was always a fire burning in the pit of the blacksmith shop. The shoes were hammered out in the fire and then dropped into a large container of water to cool down.

I'm reminded of a story about a little boy who came into a blacksmith shop to watch the smithy work. The old man had just taken a shoe out of the fire and dropped it down on the sawdust floor with the admonition, "Don't touch the shoe until it cools." The little boy was so infatuated with the process of making a horseshoe that he picked up the shoe that hadn't cooled down, and quickly threw it down again. The smithy said, "That shoe was too hot for you, wasn't it son?" The boy replied, "No sir. It just doesn't take me long to look at a horseshoe."

Jim Duncan was a religious man. He didn't go to church much, but on most Sundays you could see him sitting on his front porch, dressed in bib overalls, reading the Bible. He always whistled and sang as he worked. He often talked to himself or prayed aloud. If you walked into his shop you might think he was talking to someone. If you asked, "Mr. Duncan, how are you doing today"? He would probably reply, "Oh, we're doing just fine." Seeing no one else in the shop you might ask, "We, who"? He would then answer, "Why, me and the Lord." No matter how busy he was, he would always take time to talk to you. He was a genuine Christian gentleman, and loved by all.

RALPH JOHNSON looked more like a body builder than anything else. He was tall and muscular, and a master handyman at many trades. He worked at odd jobs all around the community. He worked for several years for the Crofton School system, serving as maintenance man, cooks helper, gofer and school bus driver. The kids loved him because he could spin some tall tales, many of which could not be substantiated. He lived past middle age and was never married. He was a fellow who would help anyone in any way he could.

Ralph Johnson occasionally drove a small school bus for the basketball team when they played games away from Crofton. We would often travel fifteen to thirty miles to play another team. It seemed like we always got a late start to the games and that forced him to drive faster than he should. Once, when the team was traveling to Lacy to play ball, the bus almost wrecked on the curve over the railroad on Highway 41 outside of Pembroke. We had been going a little too fast.

Another time, a friend of mine was hunting off the old Madisonville Road by the cemetery. He and his partner weren't having much luck scaring up quail. They suddenly heard a lot of gunfire down the road and went to investigate. Our friends spotted Ralph Johnson shooting field larks. A few days later he was in the Eat Shop bragging about how many quail he had killed. A guy sitting next to him then introduced himself as the game warden. Afraid of being arrested, Ralph Johnson then introduced himself as "the biggest liar in Crofton."

He joined the First Christian Church in Crofton where many of the school's teachers and employees attended. Soon after that he became a member of the choir. Some of my friends and I used to sit on the back pew where we could talk and see what was happening. The choir would stand up to sing and Ralph Johnson would hold the hymnal out in front of him, and it looked like he was singing at the top of his lungs. One of the choir members standing next to him said he couldn't hear him making a sound, but he put on a good performance anyway.

BEN DULIN had a shoe shop in Crofton as far back as I can remember. He was a shoe cobbler and very good at his trade. He got all the shoe repair business because he was the only business that made shoe repairs. Compared to today's prices, things were pretty cheap then. For instance, if you wanted to get your shoes half-soled, it cost about twenty-five cents for each shoe. Heel replacements cost about ten cents. Some people had steel taps placed on the heel and toe of their shoes. This not only made the sole and heel last longer, but it gave a nice sound to walking, kind of like tap dancing.

I don't remember whether Ben had a family or not. He was a jovial person, always in a good mood. When you entered his shop, he always spoke and smiled. If you needed your shoes repaired, immediately you could have a seat and wait on the repairs. The shop was always clean and smelled like shoe polish and new leather.

During these years our society was segregated, so Ben lived on the "other side of the tracks." He was probably born in Crofton and lived there all his life. He was respected and well liked by both races. I don't think most people have their shoes repaired today like they did then. I am reminded of Ben, even when I go into a shoe shop today.

ALFRED DYER was a tall, six-foot five, lanky man who walked with a five-foot stride, a very imposing figure. Dyer was an ex-marine, and a boxer for his outfit. Someone said that during World War II, they were overseas somewhere, watching a boxing match and Dyer was leading in points. This friend yelled out "Go get him!" Dyer turned around to look, but his opponent hit him and knocked him out. It was the only fight he ever lost.

Dyer was a friend to all teenagers. He worked in the coal mines on the night shift, from five o'clock in the evening to one o'clock in the morning. A lot of us to used to borrow his car to take our date out for the evening. He would always say we could use the car, if we had it back sitting in front of the DX station when he got off from work at one o'clock. He never asked anyone to put gas in his car; he would always fill it up when he got off from work. Many of us would have missed out on a lot of dates had it not been for Alfred Dyer.

One evening several of us were invited out to Dyer's house to a birthday party for his step sister, Christine. We met at the Eat Shop and walked almost a mile to the house. My second cousin, Peabody, and I walked together. All the way out to the house Peabody kept saying his foot had a blister on it, and he was limping. When we arrived Christine's father came out of the house and told us he wanted us to have a good time, but to hold our voices down because his wife was ill. We were all pretty quiet for a time, then we got to dancing and laughing and the noise was rising.

All of a sudden, with no warning, the old man came out the front door and fired a couple of rounds from his shotgun. He probably shot up into the air, but we didn't know that. All of us started running back towards town. Now I was a pretty fast runner, but when I got back to the Eat Shop Peabody had been sitting there waiting on me for about fifteen minutes. So much for the blister on his foot!

CASEY JONES worked on the L&N (Louisville and Nashville) Railroad. He was a stout, gray-haired man, who came into the barber shop every Saturday. Sometimes he would be dressed in his blue striped cover-alls and cap, but sometimes in a suit and tie. Kids would often hang around the shop just to listen to the stories the men loved to tell. Casey would come in for a shampoo, haircut, shave and shoe shine, the works. He would get a towel across his shoulder, walk over to the sink and lean over for the barber to wash his hair. Then his hair was rubbed with the towel until it was almost dry. The barber would cut his hair with scissors and a hand-held set of clippers.

He was shaved with a razor that folded up like a knife. First, a steaming hot towel was wrapped around the face and left there for maybe five minutes. This application softened the beard for easy trimming. Then the customer would step down from the barber chair, the barber would brush off the hair on his shoulders, and then rub his head with hair tonic from a tall bottle, then comb the hair and part it. Sometime during this process, the shoe shine man would be applying polish on his shoes, from the polish rubbed between his hands. After that the shine man would take this long cloth and shine the shoes back and forth with the rag popping with every twist of the hand.

The barbers were Bill Nichols and T.M Melton, my uncle. A haircut, shave and shoe shine would probably cost about fifty-cents. If there was a tip for the shoe shine man, it was usually a nickel or dime. Sometimes a "high roller" would come in and make it a quarter. Since Casey Jones was usually dressed up and spent that much money, the kids figured him to be a man of wealth, maybe a millionaire. The grooming was professional and proved to be a source of fun and excitement to the kids watching.

NICKNAMES

The small town in which I grew up was not unlike many other towns of that size. It seems that people everywhere, and for all time, had nicknames. I drew this list of nicknames from many people in Crofton I knew as a boy. If you were fortunate enough to have lived in the same time and place as I did, see if you can identify these. Answers are below.

1) Mammy   6) Boogie   11) Butterbean   15) Rabbit
2) Cubby   7) Spoony   12) Diddle   16) Hank
3) Fakey   8) Cockeye   13) Pieface   17) Worm
4) Speedy   9) Sleepy   14) Diddy   18) Arkie
5) Poordoo 10) Paddlefoot

1) Ralph Johnson; 2) Howard Martin; 3) Charles Lee Cates; 4) Billy Wagoner; 5) Clinton Clark; 6) James Wells; 7) Buddy Witherspoon; 8) Leon Dunning; 9) Herschel Dunning; 10) J.B. Renshaw; 11) Charlie Barnes; 12) Coach Bill Lile; 13) Howard Lloyd 14) Alfred Dyer; 15) Bobby Wicks; 16) Leslie Lindsey; 17) Gilbert Harrell; 18) Mose Dunning Jr.

Bill Hammonds

(L-R): Billy Wagoner, Nancy Clark, Bill Hammonds

THE OLD DAYS

As this book was being written, one of my grandsons asked, "Grandpa, what was it like in the 'old days'?" In the days of our own "Camelot" Crofton, the 40's and 50's was a different world. The average income was about $3,000 year. My dad probably made less than half that. A loaf of bread was twelve or fifteen cents. A quart of milk was close to that price. Most people always had milk in a bottle that came from a cow, unpasteurized.

Most people heated their homes from a fireplace or kerosene stove. There was no air conditioning in houses or in automobiles. One could rent a pretty nice two-bedroom house from ten to twelve dollars a month. It didn't take a village to raise a child, but every mother up and down the street felt free to correct any child when they thought it necessary. Children were taught to address their elders and parents with "yes sir" and "no sir".

Those were the black and white days if you had a television set. As I remember, Clinton and Dorothy Clark had the first TV I ever saw. I think the first TV sets were round screen with "rabbit ears". You could hardly see the picture for all the snow on the screen. There was Superman, The Little Rascals, The Lone Ranger and Tonto and many others. But the channels were few. I believe Steve Vaus penned:

> *I'd trade all the channels on the satellite*
> *If I could just turn back the clock tonight*
> *To when everybody knew wrong from right.*
> *Life was better in black and white!*

Yes, that's what it was like in the "old days" in the 40's and 50's. There were push lawnmowers, balloon tire bicycles, kool-aid powder with sugar, edible candy wax lips, and bubble gum cigars. There were peach sodas and RC colas and moon pies, Nancy Drew, Laurel and Hardy, Abbot and Costello, Sky King, The Ink Spots, The Shadow, the Phantom and Mandrake the Magician.

Dirt roads were environmentally friendly, and when it rained you could drive in the same rut for two miles. Crime was the label of meanness in large towns. The only security alarms were 22 rifles, baseball bats, and biting, barking dogs.

On a windy day you could smell turnip greens and fat back cooking a block away. You woke up about six o'clock in the morning to a breakfast of country ham, biscuits and gravy and hot coffee. If you lived on a farm, you might have cabbage, Irish potatoes, hominy, green beans and pork chops, swallowed with cold ice tea or lemonade. The big meal continued at supper with fried potatoes, chicken, corn bread, and some of the leftovers from lunch.

Webster's Dictionary defines the word "reminiscence" this way: "recalling to mind a long-forgotten experience." That's what I have attempted to do in writing this book. I've talked about people, events and experiences that can be described by the Jack Nicholson movie "As Good as It Gets." Everyone has their own lists of such experiences that come and go, many times knowing that those moments will be as good as it will get. Here are a few of mine:

- Ice skating on the mill pond
- Taking a dip in Dripping Springs
- Square dancing in Hoptown's armory
- Donkey basketball games
- Building snowmen in January
- Beating Hoptown in a basketball game
- Going to the Blue Goose Theater and sitting on plank seats
- Parking at Crofton Lake with a Dr. Pepper and a moon pie
- Riding a bike out to Joan Croft's for a party
- Gathering at the Eat Shop and punching out the punch board
- Ordering two cheeseburgers, a piece of Boston Crème pie, a Coke, then going to a movie at the Alhambra with popcorn and another Coke…all for sixty cents.

It didn't get any better than that…